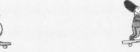

MOTHER GOOSE'S
▾ LITTLE ▾
TREASURES

MOTHER
LITTLE TR

IONA OPIE

GOOSE'S
EASURES

ROSEMARY WELLS

WALKER BOOKS
AND SUBSIDIARIES
LONDON · BOSTON · SYDNEY · AUCKLAND

INTRODUCTION

The little treasures in this book are from the far edge of Mother Goose's realm; they belong to the land of More Beyond. What I was looking for – what I hope I have found – are the most mysterious fragments from our shared memory: long-ago laughter of little meaning and echoes of ancient spells. No one knows who wrote these snatches of song; we only know that they can lift us right out of ourselves, so that we can fly high in the sky or sing with the lark in the dark – Echo! Echo! These rhymes are a confirmation that though we must live in the real world, we need to know the way to another world, where there are no limits and nothing is certain.

If I am Mother Goose's self-appointed treasurer, then Rosemary Wells is definitely her illuminator. The rhymes are as insubstantial as dreams, and as inconsequent. I put them into Rosemary's hands and she has thrown light on them. Who is the wee melodie man? A musical toad, who can play four different instruments. Why will bonny Button-cap come on a nocturnal visit? To bring the gift of a teddy bear. Why is the old dog sitting under the baby's high chair and snaffling the baby's sausages? Because he prefers them to his usual diet of stinking fish.

There is so much to discover in this book. Just turn the pages and look and listen, and say, as I do, "Oh yes, oh yes, of course!"

Iona Opie

CONTENTS

HERE COMES SOLOMON ▾ 8

THE LEAVES ARE GREEN ▾ 10

INTERY, MINTERY ▾ 12

HANDY SPANDY ▾ 14

ROSY APPLE ▾ 17

MRS WHIRLY ▾ 18

PARCEL POST ▾ 20

SING, SING ▾ 23

IN AND OUT THE WINDOWS ▾ 24

LITTLE FATTY DOCTOR ▾ 28

OATS AND BEANS AND BARLEY ▾ 30

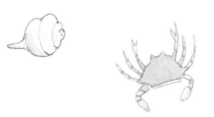

WEE MELODIE MAN ▾ 32

CHICK CHICK CHICK CHICK ▾ 34

WHAT THE GOOSE THINKETH ▾ 39

MOTHER, MAY I? ▾ 40

LITTLE OLD DOG SITS UNDER A CHAIR ▾ 42

UNCLE JOHN ▾ 44

COCKLE SHELLS ▾ 47

GOING TO KENTUCKY ▾ 48

THE MOON SHINES BRIGHT ▾ 50

MY MAID MARY ▾ 52

BEFORE IT GETS DARK ▾ 54

HERE COMES SOLOMON

Here comes Solomon in his glory,

Riding on a milk-white pony,

Up the hill in all his glory,

All for Susie's wedding:

Om, pom, Susianna, Om, pom, Susianna,

Om, pom, Susianna,

All for Susie's wedding.

THE LEAVES

The leaves are green, the nuts are brown;
They hang so high, they won't come down.

Leave them alone till frosty weather,
Then they'll all come down together.

INTERY, MINTERY

Intery, mintery, cutery, corn,

Apple seed and briar thorn,

Wire, briar, limber lock,

Five geese in a flock

Sit and sing by a spring –

"O-U-T and in again."

Handy Spandy,

sugar and candy,

French almond rock –

SPANDY

I spy a lark
Shining in the dark –
Echo! Echo!

ROSY APPLE

Rosy apple, lemon and a pear,

Bunch of roses she shall wear.

Gold and silver by her side,

She shall be a bride.

Take her by the lily-white hand,

Lead her across the water.

Blow her a kiss and say good-bye –

She's the captain's daughter.

MRS WHIRLY

Mrs Whirly sells fish,
Three ha'pence a dish.
Don't buy it,
don't buy it;
It stinks
when you fry it.

PARCEL POST

A baby and a box of pills,

A puppy and a rat,

A roly-poly pudding

And an old tomcat;

A pound of tallow candles,

And a round of buttered toast,

All came to me this morning

By the parcel post.

SING, SING

Sing, sing, what shall I sing?
Mary Ann Cotton
tied up on a string.
Where, where? Up in the air,
Selling black stockings,
a penny a pair.

IN AND OUT

I went to the ball the other night;
The ladies there were dressed in white.

THE WINDOWS

Some were short and some were tall,
And I asked God to bless them all.

In and out the windows,
In and out the windows,

In and out the windows,
Before the break of day.

LITTLE FATTY DOCTOR

Little fatty doctor, how's your wife?

Very well, thank you, she's all right.

Can she eat a tuppenny pie?

Yes, sir, yes, sir, so can I.

Oats and beans and barley grow,

Oats and beans and barley grow.

Do you or I or anyone know

How oats and beans and barley grow?

First the farmer sows his seed,

Then he stands and takes his ease,

Stamps his foot and claps his hand,

And turns around to view the land.

WEE MELODIE MAN

Here comes the wee melodie man,

The rufty tufty toady man.

I'll always do the best I can

To follow the wee melodie man.

CHICK CHICK

Chick chick chick chick chicken,
Lay a little egg for me!

I haven't had one since Easter

And now it's half past three,

So – chick chick chick chicken,

Lay a little egg for me!

Please.

WHAT THE GOOSE THINKETH

When the rain raineth
And the goose winketh,
Little knows the gosling
What the goose thinketh.

MOTHER, MAY I?

Mother, may I go out swimming?
Yes, my darling daughter;
Hang your clothes on a hickory limb,
But don't go near the water.

Little old dog sits under a chair,

Twenty-five grasshoppers

snarled in his hair.

Little old dog's beginning to snore;

Mother she tells him

to do so no more.

UNCLE JOHN

Uncle John is very sick,

What shall we send him?

Three good wishes, three good kisses,

And a slice of ginger.

What shall we send it in?

In a piece of paper.

Paper is not fine enough;

In a golden saucer.

COCKLE SHELLS

When the cockle shells turn silver bells,

And mussels grow on every tree,

When flowerets blow in frost and snow,

Then my true love returns for me.

GOING TO KENTUCKY

I was going to Kentucky,

I was going to the fair;

I met a signorina

With fandangles in her hair.

Oh shake 'em, shake 'em, shake 'em,

Shake 'em if you can,

And if you cannot shake 'em,

Do the best you can.

The moon shines bright,
The stars give a light,
And little bonny Button-cap
Will come tomorrow night.

MY MAID MARY

My maid Mary, she minds the dairy,

While I go a-hoeing

and mowing each morn;

Merrily runs the reel

And the little spinning wheel,

Whilst I am singing and mowing my corn.

BEFORE
IT GETS DARK

Down with the lambs,

Up with the lark.

Run to bed, children,

Before it gets dark.

First published 2007 by Walker Books Ltd
87 Vauxhall Walk, London SE11 5HJ

2 4 6 8 10 9 7 5 3 1

This book has been typeset in Bell Monotype

Printed in Singapore

British Library Cataloguing in Publication Data:
a catalogue record for this book is available from the British Library

ISBN 978-1-4063-1024-5

www.walkerbooks.co.uk